# You Can't Make Me Shut Up

sovereignnoir

# You Can't Make Me Shut Up

A POETRY & SHORT STORY COLLECTION

# End Time Poet

SOVEREIGN NOIR PUBLICATIONS

First paperback edition: March 2021

Print ISBN: 978-1-952987-27-4

eBook ISBN: 978-1-952987-28-1

Cover Designers: Anthony K. Gervacio
David Paul Morgan

Sovereign Noir Publications
www.sovereignnoir.com

# FOREWORD

As Jesus was getting into the boat, the man who had been demon-possessed begged to go with him. Jesus did not let him, but said, "Go home to your family and tell them how much the Lord has done for you, and how he has had mercy on you." Mark 5:18-19 (NIV)

The word of the Lord contains many types of writings. We have history, adventures, and doctrinal teaching. The book of Psalms gives us a form of worship in song and poetry. I believe the Lord gives many types of gifts to His church to bring praise to His name.

This book, "You Can't Make Me Shut Up," is a book that speaks to the gift of poetry. Throughout our history, the poetic expression has been able to bring us in close contact with our emotions and the truth of our situations. I find those principles in this book. The gift of praise and thanksgiving is evident, and the stories told by the author, Sister Kris, The End Time Poet, reveal the fact of the love and peace of God.

I love the title, as it identifies experiences of life that require a testimony.

Kris is someone who has tasted of the goodness of the Lord and needs to tell of His goodness at every turn. I am sure you will enjoy each story and poetic verse as you read. I believe you will be encouraged to discover just how good God has been to you, and then you will be able to echo the words of Sister Kris, The End Time Poet; "You can't make me shut up"!

Blessings to you, Kris on a job well done. I am proud of you!

Your Pastor,
Bishop Eric A. Lambert, Jr.
Bethel Deliverance International Church
Wyncote, PA

# DEDICATION

First and foremost, to the author and finisher of my faith, my Lord and Savior, my Father, my King of Kings, the lover of my soul who reigns on the just and the unjust, thank you for trusting me, filling my mouth, and giving me the creative ability to accomplish this project. Words bring life or death; I believe and pray that the same resurrection power that raised Jesus from the dead on the third day would also raise every person that takes the time, effort, finance, and support would be raised and encouraged to fulfill their God given destiny.

To my most loving companion, lover, friend and high priest of our loving home, King David. Only the father could manifest such a brilliant and ingenious man in my life to push me when I wanted to throw in the towel.

To Mom Veronica who believed and supported this work. Mom Veronica, not only did you talk it, you believed that God gave me a dream that would not die I appreciate and thank you so much.

To my bishop and spiritual father, Eric A. Lambert, Jr. who not only prayed, but lived the whole counsel of the Word of God. You told me long ago to make up my mind. Thank you for believing in me. Thank you Lady Lambert and family for sharing with all of us.

To Pastors Rodney and Kim Harris who counted it not robbery to be here for me during the most horrific parts of this process. You never left my side and I thank God for the both of you.

To all my praying mothers who kept me on that alter, day and night. To all my mothers who sheltered me along my walk in his service. Mom Gloria, I thank you for caring for me. Mom Darlene, Mom Brenda (R.I.P.), Mom Mornel (R.I.P.), Mom Sue Flanagan and the Kingdom Builders. God mom T.G. who never let me forget my God given gift. Mom Avery who kept that microphone in my hand. To mom Ionnie, you taught me how to love myself and to appreciate the Lord Jesus.

Pastor Valerie Travis and Minister Angie you both prayed and cared for me and I'm grateful. For I was a stranger, and you both demonstrated the Word of God and showered me with loving kindness.

My God children caused me to reach for Christ, and you've taught me so much about being a God mom. Sherell, thank you. It is an honor to be entrusted with your beautiful family. A child shall lead them!

To my B.D.I.C. family for all of your prayers and kindness. Thank you all.

To my big brother Mac Joe Soto who took me off of the streets and said, "You're my little sister and I mean it!" Mac, I love you!

To Sheena, Tracey, Angie, Paulette, Janel, Bisea, Ladies Accord, Pastor Pearl, Cheesecake Lady, and all my sisters and brothers along this journey. Thank you for all of your support and kindness.

To all those who showed up along the way, there are too many to call your names, but I thank you nonetheless.

From every child orphan in every institution (D.H.S., J.J.C., Presbyterian Children Village, Y.E.S., Catholic Social Services) to the Kirks and the Carters and all the neighbors who made each word a reality, I'm grateful to you all. I own it and I thank the Lord Jesus for you all.

To all the beautiful staff at Holy Redeemer and Allegis CARE, Abington Hospital, and Mary Joe McAuthor, I appreciate your kindness and care for me.

To all those I've wronged along the way, please forgive me. I had no right and I'm without excuse to have spoken or hurt you with my words, thoughts, or deeds. I own it all!

To everyone and tool that was used as a weapon, to every circumstance, GOD is the author and the FINISHER of my Faith...

In closing, YOU CAN'T MAKE ME SHUT UP!!!

# You Can't Make Me Shut Up

## A POETRY & SHORT STORY COLLECTION

From then until now, at times I never knew.
Now I realized all along...

# It Was You

I care about what you think
and all you have to say.
I care about spending time with you
when things don't go my way.

Even when I'm hurting
and can't understand your plans,
I still would like to sit with you
and enjoy just holding hands.

No relationship comes easy,
it takes patience, care and love,
gentleness and kindness,
commitment with lots of hugs.

You are very special,
a very loving friend, companion,
and a comforter whose washed
away my sins.

You always seem to show up
and take the rain out of each storm.
When coldness tries to steal my heart,
your word speaks and makes it warm.

You never seem to grow weary.
You never wear a mask.
You never laugh at me when I fall.
You share even when I don't ask!

You truly are my refuge, strong tower,
lover of my soul,
Father and my mother,
my King from days of old.

You are my great physician,
wonderful councilor, you're even my voice.
This breath I breathe it belongs to you
and so I will rejoice!

You amaze me with all of your beauty,
I stand in awe of you.
Captivated by your love,
I'm head over heals about you.

You are the fairest of ten thousand,
sweeter than honey in a honey comb.
The beginning and my ending,
the light to find my way home.

I'm glad my search is over,
so I can be content and just rest.
I humble myself at your feet,
no longer in duress.

Please forgive me for every betrayal,
and every time I lied to you,
turned my back and walked away when
your mercy and grace brought me through!

It was you who gave me life.
It was you who protected me.
It was you who opened up each door
when many rejected me.

It was you who gave me the talent
and you even gave me a man.
It was you who always provided the strength
when I had no courage to stand.

As I proceed to live out your story,
I just thought you should know
that every time I conquer in this land
it's you I want to show.

So I thank you for choosing me
to walk in such victory.
Thank you Jesus for giving me life
when you set the captives free!

It was you.

Why is it that I start and stop? Lord I need you!

I've been doing this all of my life, and even though I understand that you like a clean vessel inside and out, I've been to the alter, been greased up like a pizza, I've even confessed my faults. I'm not blame shifting, I enjoy this and I'm fully aware that this could kill me!

Okay, I'm gonna stop right after this!

Help me Jesus, be a light in this darkness! Where are you, and why aren't you helping me?

God I want to live for you, but I'm afraid that if you take away my weed, cigarettes, my man, liquor and all my other vices you won't give me anything back!

This is all I know, Lord!

Please help me to stop living in this...

# COFFIN WITH NO GRAVE

I made a coffin for myself, didn't need any help.
Didn't buy tools, didn't even go to school.
Don't even know how it all came about,
til I realized that I wasn't coming out!
Dust dark and gray couldn't see the light of day,
til I walked into Bethel one bright sunny day.

About seven years ago some lady pleaded with me to go,
I told that lady time and time again, Miss, I really don't know.
See I met that lady when I was in the fifth grade.
God had a plan and a foundation already laid.

I didn't know this until right about now,
I'm still learning, tryna understand how.
How I locked myself in into this coffin of sin,
Jesus let me out, but I keep goin' back in!
You see in my coffin I laid up lots of stuff:
Newports, weed, just a little bit of beer, lies, excuses,
vengeance... it was all in there!

A little black book just to have a second look
When times got tough and coming out a little rough.
This coffin has been everything in the world to me—
gluttony, sex, and self pity!
Skies turn gray and clouds turn blue,
stop looking at me stupid,
you been in a coffin too!

At times I ran out to give it all up,
ran back in didn't want God in!

When Jesus shows up something has to change,
He died and rose and bore all that pain!
Today I heard a message Jesus is coming real soon!
These are the last days that we're living in,
no more time to keep running back in!

Time to make this very important choice,
no more procrastination I heard God's voice!
It's not the first time great is His mercy for me,
He gave His only begotten Son to set us all free!
Jesus said resist the devil and he has to flee!

I don't know about you, but it's my turn.
Burning up this coffin filled with sin,
I've got this new life that I'm ready to begin!
No more sadness, sickness or disease.
Jesus gave His life for me to walk in victory!

I made a new choice today, so how about you?
My brothers and sisters,
You can burn those coffins too!
You don't have to wait to die, the devil is a lie!
Come on out, Jesus Saves!
Stop living in a coffin.

He got up from the grave!
He got up outta the grave for me and for you.
Now how about you tell those old coffins,
today we are through!

No one is listening! Can't you hear them crying?

They are being publicly humiliated, emotionally abused, and mentally tormented!

Don't you even care that the teacher who has a most beautiful smile is so crafty and that she's lying right through that gap in her teeth?

Lord, they try to make me shut up every time I open up my mouth on behalf of your children!

They are not about caring for your babies. Someone has to step in and put a stop to it.

See I can hear them, your children that is.

They're screaming sooo loud, but...

# I Do Have a Voice

God does hear my cry
So be careful of what you do
How you talk to me and
See my point of view

You can't cover up how you talk to me
You raise your voice
You always yell and seek to embarrass me

I deserve respect even at one or two
And even if my parents can't hear me
God is watching you

Oh you can say please or thank you
When you want to me to adhere
And stop making my belly ache
Causing me to be nauseous and fear

You can control your anger
Just like you want to control me
So stop allowing Satan to use you
Resist the devil and he'll flee

Stop all this talkin' about me
And then you kiss my face
You won't get away with this
God is giving you mercy and grace

Your words are forming my future
You really do have a choice
So you better repent and get some help
Cuz I do have a voice

Now I'm three and four
And you're still doing the same thing
Disregarding my feelings
And letting God's praises ring

I know you have your favorites
Cuz you always push me away
I asked you for a hug, teacher,
But you just turned and walked away

Now my heart is broken
I can't even comprehend
And when I'm with my family
You act like you love me, you pretend

Please stop hurting my feelings
And calling me out of my name
This doesn't build my character
Now my head is hung down in shame

You must get delivered
Jesus will help you through
So go back to God's alter
I know you have family and loved ones

So watch how you're handling me
Before you open up your mouth
And plant that very next seed

I'll always forgive you
Remember you do have a choice
And even if I can't tell it all
Jesus does hear my voice

Thank you for every humiliating, agonizing, painful, embarrassing, dreadful, heart-breaking moment in my life.

Thank you for never leaving, nor forsaking me.

Thank you Jesus that I can boldly proclaim that...

# I HAD TO GO WHERE I WAS AT

An overnight trip to the graveyard.
A perverted conversation with a Rite Aid security guard.
The thirty fifth district police station.
In the dark allies across the nation.
From Lima, PA. West Philly too.
Monticello, Tallahassee, Trenton, the Gallery,
Baltimore, and Ogantz Avenue.
On Good Street where I rented out the house.
In that garage on that broken down couch.

That day I hooked school and they tried to rape me.
Those abandoned houses I had to flee.
The foster care that was never really there.
The hand me down clothing that I stole everywhere.
The highways and by ways, I tried to run away.
With no where to go and no place to stay.

The floor was so cold, the food spoiled too.
Couldn't go to sleep, I had no refuge.
Diseases in my body and my teeth were rotted, too.
At ten years old, what was I supposed to do?

I tried to get help, but no one was there.
The family who adopted me truly didn't care.
They blamed it on me, said I was no good.
I now know for myself I was really just misunderstood.

This story is my life and I'm not ashamed about that.
I now know for myself that I had to go where I was at.

I didn't do things right, but I got by.
Some days I stole your money or depended on a lie.
Running around in darkness.
I always wondered why?

The love of Jesus has brought me back.
I was never abandoned,
I had to go where I was at.
Jesus kept my mind and clothed me, too.
Healed my body, I now have a refuge.
God gave me Jesus.
Some don't agree...
But Satan, you're a liar and you have to flee!

In the name of Jesus I have survived.
Even if you don't believe,
He's keeping you alive!
Jesus is Lord, He got up from the grave.
He sits on the right hand of the Father
So your soul can be saved.

They jammed nails in His hands,
lied on Him, too.
Still taking His name in vain,
they beat Him black and blue.
Jesus asked the Father,
"Do you have any other way?"
But He was still obedient,
and had no place to stay.

Jesus was rejected, acquainted with grief,
Not a spot, blemish, or wrinkle,
And yet He still decreased.

Jesus is the way truth and life,
So give up the anger, bitterness, and strife.
It's not so hard to believe.

Go ahead you do the math.
This world is coming to a end,
Only the love of Christ will last.

Confess with your mouth.
Believe in your heart.
Ask for forgiveness--
Old things must depart!

You are now without excuse,
And this is a fact.
Surrender to Jesus.
You had to go where you were at!

It's funny how a person can enter your life with the love of God in their heart.

No hidden agendas. Just wanting to lift up Jesus!

Sharing all that they own, without even a blink of an eye!

So radiant and sincere. Gentle yet strong!

Worshiping the Lord.

Always ministering in song.

Such a gift to the body of Christ.

I TRULY LOVE AND MISS YOU MY...

SISTA!

I'm so glad you're here now,
And I appreciate your gift.
The time I came for all night prayer
And you offered a 3 a.m. lift.
I've never met a woman who
Prays the whole night through.

Sister you're such a blessing,
Obedience looks great on you.
Oh yes, I've been watching
And I'm sure many others are, too.

Now, don't get nervous or fretful.
Jesus is covering you.
I love the example you're giving,
How you're free with no shame
How you seek to lift Jesus,
Not riches, popularity, and fame.

I know because you keep giving
All God gives to you,
Your time, talent, torso,
Husband and children, too.

Thank you for the basket, the rent,
The retreat, the t-shirt and the close
Attention you pay to
All your brothers and sisters
Here in the body of Christ.

Thank you for how you're teaching us
How to stay in the press and fight.

Sister, I'm not lifting you up
I give God all the praise
For sending you to help me
Come out of this baby phase.

I really didn't think I could make it.
I grow so weary at times.
I even thought to turn away
But God sent you right on time.

Thank you for being willing to suffer
And laying down your life, too.
I thank God for his Holiness
Shining so brightly on you.
So glad you rent your heart,
Not just your garment see.

I'm really thankful God has given
You as a big sister to me.

I'm going to end this poem
'Cuz I could write all night long,
But I need to get back to God's altar
Where I'll find you worshiping in song.

So you're not just my big sister
But you're my mentor, too.

Sister

Sister

Sister.


I thank God for a sister like you.

Dedicated to Pastor Delzora Terrell Poe.

How did you get here?

I must be outta my mind!

After all that has taken place, in this year alone!

Things are bad, but not bad enough for me to deceive myself into thinking that anything outside of God's will would ever go right in my life!

Thank you Jesus for the Holy Ghost.

Because Lord Jesus, you truly are my Savior.

So I refuse to keep allowing...

# STRANGERS IN MY HEART

Loneliness, rejection, fear and doubt
is how this next poem came about.
Stranger in my heart,
now what caused me to stray?
Listen and keep focused
you must hear all that I say!

You gave your only begotten Son,
Jesus, for my life.
Jesus is Lord. Say it.
It sounds so nice.

You've opened my eyes,
you made me free.
Washed me in the blood of Jesus
way back on Calvary.

I welcomed you in,
you gave me a brand new start.
Eight years later,
still I invite these strangers in my heart!

You opened my eyes, gave me a smile.
Yet your love is unconditional still all the while!
I don't read your word, don't even stop to pray!
Then when I do, still I don't know what to say!

I love you so much, but it's hard to depart,
and so I keep welcoming
these strangers into my heart.

The Newports, beer, failure, and fear.
Another twisted relationship
because I felt you weren't here.
Anger, bitterness, jealousy, and rage,
I'm not finished,
I still gotta another page!

Depression, oppression, no rest in the night.
In this armor of flesh I'm still ready to fight!
Lying and stealing rebellious everyday,
a stiff necked generation, still I can hear you say
"Come over here! It's time to draw near.
Things that are seen aren't
made from things that do appear!"

Now I don't understand, Jesus help me
to stop chasing all these false gods
in this world of idolatry!

Come out from among them,
separate yourself, touch no unclean thing.
Daughter of Zion shake yourself!
Put on your whole armor, I gave it to you!
You must read your word and observe all to do.

Helmet of salvation, I gave you a shield,
a belt, a sword, and a breast plate
you must yield!

Lord you're so faithful,
I'm thankful for another start.

Right here and right now
strangers you must depart!

In the name of Jesus, I'm never alone!
Devil you're a liar
And I'm hanging up this phone!
Jesus is my Lord, so I declare it boldly today.
I'm pulling out this poem
even when I think to stray!

It's a new season God has given you
A brand new start.
Hurry up move quickly,
evict those strangers outta ya heart!

Lord you do what you do best, and well I'm gonna do what I feel is best! This brotha is on my heels!

I'm sick of being alone. He's been pursuing me for over six months. I've been waiting for you to give me the green light on this one!

Especially since I've been obedient, I haven't been out, haven't taken any numbers, no sex, and check this out, I have even been hanging out at all night prayer.

So I know you're gonna give me a yes this time! I've gotta have him, Lord. You heard what he said, I'm gonna be his wife!

So what if he doesn't have a job? So what he's been on drugs for the lion's share of his life? This man wants me even though I'm a big girl! Men don't usually like the big girls!

His life is about identical to mines, we're practically twins. We have something in common. Oh Lord please help me, because after all that's been said and done...

# I Fell In Lust With A Dream

Five foot nine, light brown eyes,
such a gentlemen til I realized...
twenty eight days, just a short lived phase.
For over three years is what I've had to pay!

Never counted up the cost.
My own soul, could I have lost?

Got myself caught up, not so easy to go and
toss out old memories, pictures and a few,
well disobedience caused me to go through.

At first he took me out,
impressed me everyday.
Caught up with what he had to give,
but what was he taken away?

I prayed both day and night,
me and God we were so tight,
a visit or two after curfew,
still I said I'm alright!

Now all my habits change,
and this dream became deranged.

My brothers and sisters tried to help
when they saw me acting strange!

Here I stand today,
believe me Jesus made a way.

My broken heart just fell apart,
but after you suffer, you'll obey!

Still God has a plan.

It's not as bad as it may seem.

Tears and some loneliness,
but like Martin Luther King,
still I have a dream!

I'm not the only one,
hey maybe this was you.

After all that's been said and done
what is it we must do?

I'm fasting and I pray.

Reading God's word everyday.
Not doing the same things over again,
even if I think to stray!

I'm being restored right now.
Go ahead you can asked me how!
The anointing destroyed the yoke,
God backed off all them folks!

See they neva understood, my intent,
well it was all good!

My life is an open book!
Go ahead, get a real good look.

It's transparent, as if you could see,
cause Jesus heard my plea.

Now didn't you read that too,
if not Jesus made the captives free!

What is the truth in its entirety? I'm sick of pretending! Smiling and playing as if all is well! Not the truth according to humans, but what is the truth according to my Lord and Savior JESUS???

# THE TRUTH IS

The truth is I'm winning no matter what life looks like, nor how many times I fall through darkened tear filled nights!

The truth is that I'm standing, after all the standing therefore, and when my legs get worn and weak, Jesus strengthens me some more.

The truth is that I'm victorious no matter how many times I fall down, I have God's love and power, a mind that's strong and sound.

The truth is I can go on now, because old things are passed away. The truth is Jesus loves me, no matter what people think or say!

The truth is quick and powerful, gets right to the point. The truth is God's Holy word, a lie He will not anoint!

The truth is I forgive you, UN-forgiveness is nailed to the cross. The truth is total submission and counting up the cost.

Willing to surrender, laying down the self life, yielding to the Holy Spirit, ceasing from envy and strife.


The truth is that I need you, so sorry I pushed you away. The truth is I wasn't trained to listen, but always having something more to say!

The truth is I was jealous because you seemed to have it all, now I'm speaking about myself. This couldn't be you at all.

The truth is that I'm nervous and at times I'm so afraid. The truth is sometimes I've listened to the lies instead of the promises God has made.

The truth is hard to swallow when I always wanna be right. The truth should help you to repent, not walk in pride and fight!

The truth is looking in the mirror and accepting all that you see. The truth is dealing with your issues and not pointing your fingers at me!

The truth is calling on Jesus, He is a present help.

In the time of trouble, stop picking up the phone.
Call upon the name of the Lord, He'll never leave you alone!

The truth is I can make it, cause I refuse to stay this way.
The truth is crying out to God, from darkness you turn away.

The truth is God does hear you, He listens all the time. Even when we see fit to rebel, run hide, and press rewind!

The truth is Jesus is coming, in a twinkling of an eye. The truth is we better be ready, or we will do more than just die!

The truth is Jesus is Lord, so tear those fleshly idols down.

The truth is in those sixty six books we call the Holy Bible!

The truth is you better read it and observe to apply God's word! The truth is we do know better, so repent and do all you've heard!

The truth is sorry won't help when we keep doing the same ole thing! Then offer God some filthy worship, and keep letting his praises ring!

The truth is God has mercy, but be careful not to provoke. We also better be careful of how we handle God's folks!

The truth is that I'm finished, won't write another line. The truth is I'm grateful for you, the readers, and you keeping the Lord Jesus in mind!

That's the truth!

On the phone with my lover and best friend, chitting and chatting about this and that, until he asked me to get quiet so I could write down all that I could hear.

On the throne of my heart, sitting in my Father's seat, was all of this stuff. I was bound and not free! The phone, the people, all of the cares of this life, the unforgiveness and much strife.

In the Bible I read a story about a statue people praised. It was a false god the people had raised. In my perception and from my point of view, Dagon had to go.

It was time for me to choose!

# DAGON

Always on this phone taking up my breath,
don't wanna be lonely, don't know how to rest.

I'm scared of what I'll hear, don't know what I'll see,
don't know what I'll say, just don't wanna know me!

Gonna hang up dis phone, right after this next line.
The phone is not my God, I've been the walking blind!

Jesus is my Lord, just thought you should know.
Spend some time with Jesus and let the vices go!

Goodbye, I'm getting off this phone!

The preachers in the church serving the daily bread. We call it God's Word, proclaiming Jesus is alive and not dead!!!

The seats have been filled. I've made up my mind, no more fighting. Jesus I need you I...

# JUST WANNA GET IT RIGHT

Yesterday I cussed out a neighbor. They had abused me for over ten years. You would think that I felt bad, but I didn't even shed one tear!

Even as I'm sitting here writing, I'm laughing about it in my heart. Because she as well couldn't believe it, she was in shock that I threw back a dart!

This story is far from over, and what I must say next, is that I'm a servant of Jesus, not at all what one would expect.

My words were not at all seasoned. My attitude did not represent the shows I've been watching on TV, well I guess you know where my time has been spent.

Lord, please forgive me. My words weren't seasoned, nor few. Wash me in the blood of Jesus, please, show me what to do.

You already know my daughter, just get up and get it done! Jesus died for this very reason, remember the victory has already been won!

The righteous fall down, and get back up.

No more sleeping all throughout the day. Take up thy bed, get on your knees and pray.

As you take time the Lord Jesus will fill your cup. My brothers and sisters it's time to...

# GET UP

This life stands still for no one,
betta get up outta this bed
of loneliness, fear, and anxiety.
Empty those dreams up outta ya head!

Wait for someone to reach for you?
Blame the mother that bore you?
Make another excuse instead of taking
heed of all the examples before you?

Betta get up outta this bed,
keep making you eyes turn red.

Stuck on stupid and angry
cuz you pretend you
ain't heard what I said!

Now you betta get up from dis pool,
waiting for somebody to put you in.
Blaming it on the situation, you betta
make Jesus your life long friend
and get up outta this bed!

Take up thy bed and walk!

# I Surrender All

I have not written in a while, often times I feel I'm slipping away. This cross I bear gets heavy and this pain seems to stay.

My mind gets foggy with circumstance, my heart hardens from worry and stress. My life is shattered in trillions of pieces, my dreams in a total mess.

How do I push to press forward? Just how do I obey at all times? How do I stop sounding like a broken record or a screeching tape stuck on rewind?

My weight is at a record high, all of my family has faded away. Whatever happened to how it was supposed to be, consumed with grief all along, still I pray.

How do I have hope and believe you, when I've made a mess of my life? My choices have plagued me with death, but when I called on my Savior Jesus, I could stop grasping for breath.

You've given me drink in this desert, a refuge from the elements. Even the rain. You continuously bathe me in the Blood of Jesus, consumed me in your love to provoke change!

You're the lover of my soul, the one constant I just can't ignore. You keep filling me with your Spirit, shielding me from all that has happened before!

I've reached my hands back in the fires, I've even slapped your face. I've even had nerve to cuss and lie as you extended more mercy and grace.

I've taken each moment for granted and yet you've still seen me through. My master, Lord, and Savior, it's time for me to trust in you!

I surrender each part of my being, the one thing that I can do right. I repent from every abomination. I surrender, Lord, to your will tonight!

# Who Told You That?

Who told you that it was okay to live this life your way, to disregard God's Holy word cause children don't have to obey?

Who told you that you could get by with just another lie, break every rule, drop outta school, and you don't even have to try?

Who told you that it was alright to stay out half the night, talk on the phone cause you think you are grown, and when corrected you're ready to fight?

Who told you that life would be easy? That you wouldn't have to go through. When your family no longer believes in you, now you're running after a boo!

Who told you that he would love you and be there to hold your hand when he's probably tryna get close enough to get you to drop those pants!

Who told you that when you get angry, that it's an excuse to be rude, and when God sends correction, here comes your attitude!

Who told you that you can go on sitting in back of the church, chew your gum, play with your cell, and answer your chirp?

Who told you that you don't have to listen cause adults are sometimes wrong, too? Instead of dealing with their issues, it's easier to keep checking you!

Who told you that God doesn't hear when you cry in the midnight hour? Christ is calling you higher, so you too can walk in his power!

Who told you that you're not important and to have your head hung down in shame? Just because you messed up big, you don't have to wallow nor remain.

Who told you that God doesn't love you because nothing seems to go right? Remember, the Bible and what God says, that the just don't walk by sight!

The adversary's name is Satan, he's the father of all lies. He sits right up on your shoulders covering up your eyes! He wants you to give up your body, to stay in the mirror too. He wants you to focus on all things that distract and feel good to you!

He wants you to wear tight clothing, he wants you to chase girls or boys. He wants you to disregard all you've been learning. Drown it out as if it were just noise!

Yeah you came out tonight, but exactly why are you here? Because your parents forced you, come chill with your friends, cause the end isn't coming it's here!

The Lord really has need of you, no matter what has taken place. He wants you to get to know him. He's given you mercy and grace.

You are important and we need you in the body of Christ, so please repent and come closer. It's time to give God your life!

The fashion show is over. The curtain comes down this day. The next time you hear those voices, lift up your head and say, "Lord I really do need you, no matter what I say or do, I'm crying out for you to save me. I'm ready to surrender to you!"

When your heart has been broken and you're on the wrong track, please remember this poem and ask yourself, "who told you that?"

So often I'd just open up my big mouth and say it!

It didn't matter how I would sound, or even whom my words would affect.

If I felt you needed it, best believe you were a perfect candidate for my opinion!

Forget about timing and tack or etiquette.

If you were getting on my nerves, well, I just felt completely justified in letting you have a piece of my mind.

Til one day someone bought me some of the most scrumptious gossip and out of no where...

# I Thought Before I Spoke

It was different this time
I didn't just open up my mouth
I paused for a brief moment

I thought about what I really wanted to say
Since it didn't glorify God instead of speaking
I thought to pray

Now this even took me by surprise
Excited beyond measure
Words can't begin to verbalize

I knew it was my God at work
For me to pray instead of sounding
Like some insensitive jerk

Yeah, it definitely was the Holy Ghost
Cuz what I've always loved the most
To share my opinion, be it wrong or right

On a lot of my words I had to choke
Not this time y'all
Cuz I thought before I spoke

To glorify God even in my voice
Taking time out to think
And using words of choice
The room was so quiet

They waited to hear what I had to say
They were very disturbed when I said
"I'll just pray"

It was the power of God
That cause me not to say
what was on my mind

I could hear those words so loud in my heart
But in that same moment
I was given a brand new start

Love covers a multitude of sins
Jesus only knows how the story starts
And where it all ends

In the book of James
Chapter 3, in the sixth, seventh, and eighth verse
It speaks of our tongues
How they are wicked and perverse

Out of one mouth
How can we bless and then curse

Let's get right saints
Cuz it ought not be
There is no fountain producing
Both bitter and sweet

Our words can bring life
or kill to some degree
I'm talking to you
But starting with me

I was so thankful
I really must say
I didn't just speak
But I was led to pray

I thought before I spoke today

I've made up my mind so many times before.

I'm just not gonna do things the same 'ole way expecting a change! Life has to be more than just failures and defeats, moments of imaginary victories.

See I was so proud of the new decisions I've made.

Now, come to find out when things don't go my way, I'm doing the same things over just on a different day!

Well...

I'M DONE

I'm done compromising God's will for my life,
vacillating back and forth from darkness into light!
I'm done making excuses so I can live this life my way,
when God is the living potter, and I am truly his clay.
I'm done pleasing people, betraying God to please my flesh.
When Jesus made a way for me to delight in God and rest.
I'm done looking back, when Jesus made me free. From fear,
rejection, failure and doubt, bondage and captivity!

I'm done being a wimp, it's time that I go forth.
Dressing in the whole armor of God,
knowing that the battle is fought!
I'm done feeling guilt and sorrow
for all the mistakes I've made,
when all my footsteps were ordered
before the foundation was ever laid!

Even disobedience God already factored that in,
and so He gave His Son Jesus who died and rose again!
I'm done listening to you, myself and Satan too,
when God can never lie, so I must listen to Him and do.
Everything God said, in black and white and red,
keeping in remembrance the book of
Psalms three, that He's the lifter of my head!

Now I'm done wearing these grave clothes,
when I've been given a robe of pure white,
a covenant and a comforter,
for those dark and lonely nights.

I'm done with all these tears,
cause it didn't work out my way.
My spirit, soul and mind rejoice
for brand new mercies in a brand new day!
I'm done contemplating just how to kill myself,
I'm calling on my Savior Jesus,
in this trouble He is my present help.

I'm done giving up my body
just to have some relationship,
and because Jesus is my healer
when I walk by, I don't even trip!
I'm done with worry and anxiety,
designed to take my mind.
Peace be still in the name of Jesus,
uh-uh devil not this time!

I'm done with unforgiveness
I'm releasing you right now,
I don't even have to forgive on my own,
Jesus will show me how!
I'm done living a life substandard
to God's Holy will, when I can seek first the Kingdom
and every promise God will fulfill.
I'm done blaming my issues on what happened
when I was eight or nine!
When Jesus put a new taste in my mouth.
Try it, it's a new wine!
He removed that cup of trembling
far away from  me,
He'll do it for you if you stop running too,

confess, repent and agree!
I'm done walking on egg shells
because you don't like me
and with Jesus in my corner
I've got the victory!

I'm done changing my being
so your lifestyle I can live.
I'm made in the image of Jesus Christ
who suffered, died, and lives.
I'm done looking for approval
for who I am and how I should be.
I'm made in the image of Jesus
fearful and wonderfully!

I'm done feeling defeated
I walk in victory everyday.
God shut the mouth of the naysayers
and has made a open display!

So I give God all the Glory,
for the poem inside this story.
I'm now done writing this poem
and I hope you will agree.
Be done and resist the devil,
and watch that liar flee!

Just fed up going around the mountain over and over again.
Seems like the harder I push I just can't seem to win.
I've focused, I've cried, I've pushed myself to the edge to the
point where I have just wanted to jump over the ledge.

Finally, I realized I had to sit still and cry out to Jesus,
and learn His will. Now I understand this outrageous
condition. See it's okay to start over, nothing wrong
with...

# REPETITION

I've tried this all before, over and over again, but the more I go forth, the faster I slip back. Just can't seem to keep this monkey off my back.

I've tried to eat right, go to bed on time, stop thinking about sex, or this hill I gotta climb.

I hoped, I dreamed, even sat in that church, forgave all of them folks that never saw what I'm worth!

I tried the truth and A.A. too, I tried confession, even tried getting me a boo! I tried weed, tried to be a thief, I tried to be popular it just bought me more grief. I've tried the pills, tried the bars, I tried self pity, and none of them got me very far!

I changed my clothes, cut loose the scrubs, I tried an extra nine to five, I tried man's love. I just fell on my face over and over again, but when I tried Jesus I had hope to try again.

Although I still fall down and sometimes I don't know what I'm gonna do, when I call the Name of Jesus His love and power brings me through!

The more I tried, the more I fell, cause all the while I neglected to try Jesus. He'll never fail!

Every time I put one foot in front of the other, every time I climb another step, every time I press to push forth.

Something in my mind keeps tryna snatch me back into a place of dread, doubt, fear and defeat!

Every time I set a goal short or long term that is my feet get tangled in torment! I'm not five any longer!

I'm living on my own.

Old things are passed away.
Jesus came to make the captives free!
Whom the Son has made free is free indeed!

Sooo....

# Before Doesn't Matter Anymore

I can't go forward always looking back,
before is over right now is where I'm at.
Before is a trick a trap to take my mind.
It's good to remember, but
not all day nor all the time.

Before I was an orphan,
a wayward child if you will.
I'm now a member of the Body of Christ,
so before peace be still!

Before I was homeless,
I hung around in the park.
Right now Jesus is my light,
even after dark.

Before is filled with desperation,
defeat, death and doubt,
but right now I'm safe and secure
because Jesus continues working it out!

Before I was rejected,
despised by almost every man,
right now Jesus is my Lord
and that's why here I stand!
Before I wanted vengeance
for all they did to me,
but right now I bless them,
that curse, and pray for my enemy.

Before I was ashamed
and I took on all the blame.
I now know that Jesus is my Lord
who suffered, died, and reigns!

Before I was afraid
I just didn't know how to go on,
but Jesus picked me up,
carried me along the way,
washed me in His precious blood and
has given me something to say.

Before I was a liar, a thief and a victim too.
I slept around no peace to be found,
just didn't know what to do!

I can go on and on about all that happened before,
but in the NAME OF JESUS I must shut the door!
Before is in the passed and old things are passed away.
It's time to go forth IN THE NAME OF JESUS
in search of a brighter day!

Cause before doesn't matter anymore!

I've been invited to this event for about two or three years. I'm shaking like a leaf. I can't hold back these emotions and tears. I must take a stand time to depart.

Bow down thy ear as we have this...

# HEART TO HEART

Come close and listen, now bow down thine ear. It's the love of our Lord Jesus that's why we've gathered here.

Your clothes look so nice, now check out those shoes, but I've created you with a purpose and it's time for you to choose!

No more procrastination, no more straddling the fence. No more of your own agendas. You were not sent, you just went.

You say that you love me, but will you obey? I've given you my all and yet you still go astray!

I've called for my lovers, but where are you now? Still making excuses, when it's time to lay your life down!

Lay aside every weight, surrender your all. Prepare for I am coming the proud you will fall!

Come out from among them, separate yourself. It is I who brought you out into this land full of wealth.

I've stretched fourth my hand for I love you so much. That's why I sent my son Jesus, you need more than a touch.

I will not be mocked, my sheep please hear what I say, repent and come close for calamity is on the way!

Harden not your hearts, turn from your wicked ways. It's still not to late for I have made a way.

Seek first my Kingdom, you've heard it all before. Yet time after time you continue to ignore!

My servants have spoken, I've sent them to you. The time is at hand and again I say choose!

I have not forgotten, my word just can't lie, Jesus is returning in a twinkling of an eye!

You must forgive, as I have forgiven you. Lean not to your own understanding, put your trust in me. Take up your cross and follow after Me.

Move quickly while I'm still calling, no more time to play. Take fast hold of my instruction, it's time to fast and pray!

Put on your whole armor, tare those idols down. Rent your hearts not just your garments, the wise I will confound!

Remember that I love you. From this present world you must depart. My mercy endureth forever, that's why we've had this heart to heart!

My sheep hear my voice.

# WHO AM I?

Who am I? Well I thought I already knew,
but when my past was stripped from me
and my gifts and talents too?

This revelation kinda blew me away,
I mean I really didn't know what to think, or say!
My gifts are nice, and my art work to,
but who I am is not what I do!
Are you getting this? Well it took me a while,
to separate self from form, fashion and style,
negativity, critics and my environment,
that's not who I am, but where I was sent!

Name, age, height and weight,
a few indicators but not my fate!
Stop! Wait a minute! I've figured it out!
These next few lines erased all doubt!
God made me, and He made you too.
Jesus over came and brought us through!

So who am I you still have to ask?
I'm a child of God, fearfully and wonderously made.
Whose promise won't fade, now tell me,
who are you?

# SCATTERED

PRAYER doesn't change people, it changes you.
You will go as far as you believe.
Get to know Jesus, then work for Him.

GOD didn't call us to Church work,
He's calling us to relationship!

Do you want to know Jesus, or about Him?
You fall down because you have the ability to walk.
The just live by faith, they don't respond to faith.
Confess, repent, believe!
People who put on masks never get help.

IF we love JESUS we should mimic Him.
Do you have a relationship, or a religion?
Try the spirit by the Word.
DON'T allow people to dictate your response.

Character is what you have.
Reputation is what people think of you!


Dedicated to Bishop Eric A. Lambert Jr.
Thank you for sharing the Truth.

# SCATTERED II

The will of God won't lead you
Where the grace of God won't keep you

My name is on the rock and
I'm standing on the roll.

The Lord will be the hope of
His people, not man
Until you act on God's word
You don't believe Him!

GOD has issued a warning
You heard Him
Get right or get left
How is a faith buster
There is time in a breath

When the rapture comes
you can have my half of hoagie... lol

Fear anything that takes you away from the word of God

When you need to be reassured time and time again and been hearing negative speech from your relatives, neighbors and your friends, the Lord is so faithful. He's sure to give you a special token.

Remember when everyone else doesn't have the answers you desire. The Lord...

# GOD HAS SPOKEN

I'm on this brand new road, yes I'm on my way!
Jesus lifted me, my Lord brought me along way.

My shoes are not worn out. My eyes are shining bright.
My smile is in place.

My mind is at rest tonight!

My head is lifted, my heart is clean?
My Jesus is alive, do you know what I mean?

They said I would die, that I didn't have a chance,
but the game was rigged and so I dance like David danced!

Now I had many doubts, my tears cried a flood.
My faith was worn. I was stuck in the mud!

I listened to the crowd, and all of life's noise,
the laughter and snares of many girls and boys!

I wanted to vanish, hide just disappear,
but Jesus my Lord said "it's time to draw near!"

He promised to heal me, he told me he cared.
He said only believe me and stay over here.


He kept on whispering deep in my heart,
telling me to trust him and never to depart!

He said for me to obey and never to give up,
He said I have favor and an overflowing cup.

He said that I'm chosen and I am his friend.
He said for me to live, bow down, and repent.

He said only believe and stay in my word.
He said never depart and to do all you've heard!

He said that He has not forgotten, He said that He cares.
He said I'm your healer and that I've heard every prayer.

He said it's not over, He said that I win.
To trust and believe cause He's coming back again!

I am He who lives and breathes,
I am not mocked, don't be deceived!

I am here you mustn't doubt,
I am alive and I've worked it all out!

I am the beginning and the end.
Can you hear me? I'm talking my friend.

My sheep hear my voice and another
Shepard they will not follow!

It takes transparency and courage with a mind and heart to cry out. You gotta believe the Lord Jesus. No room for unbelief and doubt.

The truth will make me free. Yes it's time to depart from opening up your mouth and...

# Lying With A Sincere Heart

I really do mean it so I can get what I want. The truth would cause me to raise the standard and cause me to submit to the will of God.

I'd rather keep manipulating, deceiving, wounding, and hurting one of God's children, or creation.

After all you know, someone did it to me. Besides if I pull off all of these mask I won't be accepted for who God has called me to be.

I don't intend to wound you, but this is in fact comfortable for me. To inflict pain upon you, so I won't have to sacrifice me!

After all, you know God understands me. To walk in the past, when I'm free at last. No more excuses time to go to class?

Renew my mind, wake up on time, tell the whole truth and stop all this lying, with a sincere heart, when I've been given this brand new start.

Read God's word, do what I've heard. Step up to the plate and stop being scared!

Repent, confess and in my heart believe. Stop sliding back, press towards the mark and achieve! No more turning left, nor right.

Keeping my eyes on the prize, cause I now realize, what Jesus said, Take up thy bed. Stop the self pity and lift up my head!

Jesus gave his life, so I could be free, sent his Holy Spirit to lead and guide me, into this light, giving me sight!

Still teaching me to live. Instead of taking, now I'm learning how to give. What the Lord has given, Jesus has given to me. To walk in His truth, power and total victory!

Taking advantage of this brand new start, standing in the truth, no more lying with an sincere heart! God's changing my mind, attitude too, I'll say it again. There's just no limit to what Jesus can do.

The same yesterday, today and forever. We are all without excuse when we say never, will we change acting all strange, continuing on a path confused and deranged.

Could it be, just a harsh reality, to stay in a darkness quite comfortable you see! We are all without excuse, the stories don't matter. Start calling out to Jesus and stop the chit chatter!

Make a new choice, I dare you to depart, from opening up your mouth lying with a sincere heart!

Taking every moment for granted.

Not focused on each seed that was planted,

not turning my head left and right.

Realizing the just walk by faith and not by sight.

Same television shows, parties and games.

Making bad choices looking for someone else to blame.

You better dig on this cause this just ain't no fancy rhyme.

Ya see JESUS is coming back and there's just...

# No More Time

No more time to be cooking lots of food. Reading and praying only when you're in the mood. Mad as hell always ready to fight, tryna figure out whose got it wrong or right.

Polishing up your act, switching up your mask. When it comes to your whole armor, well don't you even ask! Is it in the closet, or up under a chair? And you wonder how some crept in while you were unaware!

No time to fellowship with Jesus, cause I just gotta have the mic. Ministry is your God, not the Lord Jesus Christ!

Oh yeah, I see you praise me in the middle of the crowd, but when we're home alone, praise isn't turned up so loud. Depart from me, you that work iniquity. I told you to repent, come follow, and agree.

All of your good works won't help you make it in, seek ye first my Kingdom and you'll be sure to make it in! Draw nigh unto me, I'll draw nigh unto you, death won't even stop me. I'll be sure to raise your roof!

Don't you hear the sound? The urgency is in the air, but when I look into your hearts it's as if you don't even care!

You love me with your words, but your hearts are dead with sin. All because I deliver you and you decide to run back in! The day you hear me knocking, open up to me, I love you very much and I've come to set you free!

You are just a vapor, here one day and gone the next. Still you hold sin like a gun. It's a game called Russian roulette.

First, you place a bullet in the chamber of a gun. Spin the barrel, pull the trigger, now let's see if you have won.

No more time for games or breaking all the rules, lazy, unforgiving, pretending that you choose. I'm rounding up the saints, separating the wheat from the tare casting out all ain'ts.

Today you've heard me calling, another personal invite. Come on you must move quickly, no more time to fight!

The road has not been easy and everything you will not understand. My child it's time to trust me. It's time to take hold of my hand!

I bid you to come, surrender your all at the cross. Jesus is the answer so that your soul it won't be lost.

Again, I love you very much, you are no longer the walking blind. My arms are open to you. There is truly no more time!

# I Can't Reach It

I can't reach it, the roots of the rot.
The jealousy and envy cause of what others got.
The deadly deceptions, the dark desires, the pride,
And perceptions that will land you in the fire.
The malice and manipulation making me sick
Cause instead of surrender it seems easier to trick.
The easy way out, the lies that just lay.
Lord I can't reach it and Jesus is on the way.
The bad attitudes, the talks that take a toll
Hindering my deliverance on my quest to be made whole.
I just can't reach the root to the branches on these trees
That cause me to waiver back and forth,
Causing me to buckle at the knees.

The late night meals in pursuit to comfort the pain,
But instead I'm left in torment in some devastating hurricane.
Drinks can't help me, nor Facebook friends.
Jesus is the key and so here I go again
Making more room in hopes of more change
Instead of falling off with behavior that's deranged.
These roots are so rotten, hiding deep within
And yet you say you love me
And that I'm now called your friend.

I just can't reach the roots where I choose not to forgive
And so I wear this mask that smiles and helps me live
In a pseudo world amongst the pseudo crowd.
And instead of just repent and turn, I'm busy and just loud.
Lord Jesus I'm tired now and I heard you have a way
For me to live new life. Here I am today.
Take me as I am, wipe away these tears,
Paralyzing thoughts brought on by false fears
Lord I've read your word
Jesus is the truth
I heard that you will provide
As you were there for Naomi and Ruth,
Noah and the ark,
Jonah and the whale,
Abraham and Sarah who told a tall tale,
Daniel in the den,
Those three thrown in that fire,
Paul knocked off the horse,
even Judas and he was a liar.

Lord I know you love me. It's you who try the hearts in.
So I have no shame you quench the fiery darts.
Instead of throwing a fit, I'm seeking you and I sit
Calling out to you lord cause I can't reach it.

I surrender all.

# I'm Still Standing Here

No stockings, no home, the streets I had to roam.
Some laughed, others cried.
My being was denied,
But I stood and I stayed, and still I take this stand.
Jesus made a way.
I'm holding God's unchanging hand!

See I was small then got fat,
Saints got fed up and turned their backs...
But I stayed and I prayed
God has opened up my ears, canceled all my debts,
That's why I'm still standing here.

I'm being taught that only God's word can stand.
I'm learning to lean on Jesus, not some tall handsome man.
I have hope and I can cope even when I mess up bad.
It really doesn't matter whether I'm happy or I'm sad.
Now I've been drunk and I've been broke, even was a thief.
Master at self pity. Being a liar, I was the chief.

Been made to face lions, and tigers, and big ole grizzly bears,
But check this out y'all,
That's why I'm still standing here!

Okay that's enough cuz old things are passed away,
But wait a minute y'all, there's something else that I must say.

Jesus picked me up and He lifted up my head,
Still filling me with His Holy Word
And just in case you haven't heard,
I have a home. I'm not alone.
Jesus paid it all.

When I'm standing upright, but just in case I fall,
He's given His angels charge over me.
I'm still here marching on in victory!

See I was down, but never out.
Jesus won that final bout.

Opened my eyes, I now realize why Jesus gave His life.
I am proud. That's why I'm loud, you can join me too.
We're here today. Jesus paved the way and you're still
Standing here too!

# The Only Winning Team

My dream is just so big.
It reaches way past my life.
I've envisioned the trucks and
the planes way up past the sky!

No ordinary stores,
or money to go and shop!
When it's said and done,
many jaws are gonna drop!

Since the age of six,
my dreams continue to grow.
Since Jesus is my life source,
he'll make and open show!

To give God all the glory and
me the braggin rights of
how he invaded darkness and
shines this great big light!

My Savior and my King,
master and my ruler,
Lord of everything!

Fed over five thousand,
turned the water to wine.
If He did it way back then.
I just know He'll do it with mine!

It's gonna take a miracle,
to accomplish all I see and
like Joshua and Caleb,
I believe and agree!

Now I've spent many
days and nights
crying and feeling ashamed.
Instead of celebrating and
rejoicing I took on all this blame!

See they said I never make it.
Many enjoyed watching me cry,
but God said you shall live
and your dreams will never die!

So many walked away,
others shook their heads,
but God spoke daughter get up!
Only believe what I said!

Now what I love the most
about my story and my dream
is the game was already fixed,
Jesus is the winning team!

I was never alone.
He sent many to assist and stay.
I just had to be patient,
stay on my wall, and pray!

It took so many days and hours.
Some days I had worry and doubt.
Instead of walking in faith,
I wondered when it would all work out!

I lived under poverty, anxiety, and
insomnia seemed to be my friend.
Spent so much time being angry and jealous,
yup I know it was a sin!

God sent his mercy,
topped with heapings of grace.
Then He gave me a comforter,
taught me how to endure in this race.

Now my eyes are opened.
My head is never hung down.
My smile is bright and widened.
My Lord has turned things around!

To all my brothers and sistas,
to all those that do have a dream.
Surrender your life to Jesus, and
remember He's the winning team!
Never give up!

You know the answer, just open up your ears. You've heard it all before and if not , this is your year.

Look at all the devastation all across the nation. Jesus is thee answer. He's offering us all...

# LIBERATION

My Father, I don't ever mean to just shut you out.
But I've been so afraid and I have lots of doubts.
The thought of hospitals make me sick,
I don't care for doctors, pills nor tricks!

Needles and knives, yes I'm ashamed!
It's all my fault I have no one to blame.
My body is sore, and my legs feel weak.
I'm not really certain of just how to speak!

I'm really embarrassed and I just want to disappear.
Most of the time I just can't feel you near!
Can you just fix it? All of my wrongs?
Make me whole, sound, and strong!

Shrink my body, remove all of this fat.
Heal my knees, feet, and back!
Fix my mind, mend my heart.
Lord, let's you and I have a brand new start.

I've made a big mess, forgive me again.
Wash me in the blood Jesus my friend!
Turn it around, please lift my head.
Lord please have mercy, I'll take up my bed!
I need you Lord to break me out,
give me a song, dance and a shout!
I'll tell the world, of how you made me free.
From a life of death and poverty!

Save me Lord all over again.

I welcome you Jesus, I invite you in.
I believe it's time for me to rise.
Wipe this self pity out of my eyes!

I'm learning to trust you and Lord I do believe.
I'm letting go of the anger, that I may receive.
All that you've promised, help me be still,
I'm not crying wolf, Jesus I am for real!

Here I am daughter, I've waited for your call.
The symptoms and signs, don't mean much at all.
Believe my report, do what I say.
Sit in your seat, you must obey!

Keep on writing. Always forgive.
It's in me. Do you, breathe, move, and live.
It's a new season, you will succeed.
I'm gonna bless you with all that you need!

Relax and rest, stay in my word.
Let go of the fears and all that's absurd!
Reach out to me, everyday press.
Surrender those burdens piled high on your chest!

I've called you to liberty, victory and peace,
purity and wholeness to say the least.
Lift up that head! Put a smile on that face!
Endure hardness like a good soldier.
You'll finish strong in this race!

Focus, come close, mark this day.
I'm you're healer, do what I say!
Shout for joy, sing your song.
Stop living in the past, your mind is strong!

My darling child, apple of my eye.
Be confident, be strong, for it is I!
Walk with me, remember I can hear.
I am your comforter and always near!

There is an hour where no man can work!
It's time to seize the moment.
Time wasn't promised to any of us.
It's time to push, press, focus,
repent and believe all God has spoken.

In unity we shall capitalize on every...

# OPPORTUNITY

I've been given the opportunity to live another life.
The previous one is over thanks to Jesus Christ!
I'd be a fool to live life the same way.
This time life will be different because this time I'll obey!
The doctor visits make me nervous.
At times the dentist have made me afraid.
I still go forth with my head up with courage.
I'm being brave!

Everyday I'm in the shower.
I clean my home more and more.
I try to remember to take the trash out and
put both locks on the door.
I always flush the toilet and
don't eat in my bedroom.
I vacuum and sweep the hallways
to get good use outta that broom!
I wash my clothes every week.
I brush my teeth twice a day,
I even read my Bible and
I really love to pray.

One day these things will be easy,
at present these things are a task.
No longer am I a little girl,
more than twenty years have passed!
Yes, I am so grateful and
thankful for each day.
At first I really hated God
for bringing me up the rough way!

The young girls in my neighborhood
went in the house about eight or nine.
I just hid in the bushes or slept on
porch furniture half the time!
At eight I discovered my entire family
abandoned me and the people who were
supposed to raise me were a complete mess.
They beat me and showed so much hatred,
never thought to apologize!
At the age of ten or eleven I began to realize.

If I was ever to make it I had to leave this town,
it was never my intention to get diseases
from men passing me all around!
I would work long hours
in and out of relationships.
Trying hard to be accepted even tried
to do magic tricks!
I was despised in society,
tortured and bruised all the time.
I'm amazed that I'm still breathing,
thought I'd never live passed nine!
When you don't know a persons story,
you really shouldn't throw stones,
shake your head and talk about them
as you go back to your fancy homes!

At present I'm in therapy.
Mary Joe really is cool.
She said I was a very strong trauma victim

who has broken so many rules!
I've never been on pills,
and never touched cocaine.
Didn't drown in lots of alcohol to
alleviate all of life's pain!
Faith comes by hearing.
The word of God is so true.
If God can mend my broken life,
He'll do the same for you.
One day I'll get married
and have a couple of kids,
keep it moving forward
not focused on all I did!

To God be all the Glory,
my Lord Jesus Christ.
He left me as a witness.
Yup, He's given me
the bragging rights!
Jesus loves me so much
and I know that He loves you too.
Come on out and give Him your heart
because there's much room for you!
Today it is a good day,
because you too are alive.
Jesus brought you all this way,
He helped you to survive!
He canceled the death
assignment on your life,
Jesus is alive!

Don't you want to make it?
Anger is not the way.
Just call out to Jesus Christ,
He's already made away!
It's going to take some time,
don't give up cause things look bad.
Stop rehearsing all those memories
that made you feel like trash!
Today is your opportunity,
just continue to take another step.
Jesus has made you free.
Don't stare at your neighbor,
this one is just for you.
Look at all the tears you've cried and
all that you've been through.

Okay I'm wrapping it up.
I'm just so happy to see that
Jesus came to give you new life.
This is your opportunity!

# THE SOUND

Out of my window you can hear the pain of the guys standing so near. Some with STDs kicked out of their homes. Chillin' by their cars, always on the phone.

They have a certain time they just pour out their hearts. Some like to fight and throw fiery darts. Some wanna sound cool like they got it made. Some so quiet nervous and afraid.

Chicken wings, pizza, sodas and brews, waiting for half naked sistas to slide on through! Some from the hood or around the way. Some from down North came to play.

The courts across the street, some sit in the park. Some waiting to creep half pass dark. I feel really bad about all that I hear, at times I start to pray, so I just pull up a chair.

They have no idea that I'm sitting right above, shedding my tears pouring out God's love. I hear lots of words that cut so deep, at times I can't read or even fall asleep.

They call women tramps and whores, even call many female dogs walking on all four! Eight million stories in the middle of the night, about how they sold all their drugs or screwed a sista just right.

Some God's sons and His creation too, I use to get angry til I learned what I had to do.

See I use to cuss, light up my weed, perform for the brothas that talked about me. Drink up the beer, wear tight clothes, did everything besides put crack up my nose!

How did I get help, what turned me around? Well it wasn't well meaning saints wit their nose turned down.

I've gotta plan and I'm starting today, all the brothas need is for us to cry out and pray! Speak a kind word, that's what helped me. Not gossip and suggestions with no sincerity!

Some brothas were raped, their father's left them too. Some still hurting from all the childhood abuse.

A single mom working two or three jobs, hungry for food and so they sold drugs or robbed! So what we know the problems, what are we willing to do? Jesus is the answer, God does have a plan, the prison system can't turn a boy into a man!

Saved single brothers and the married men, go out into God's vineyard, show them how to make it in.

Take out some time from daily routine, give back what was free. My sistas we can make a difference too, don't just get angry and get an attitude!

Some of us were all messed up from around the way, it was God that sent His love that taught us not to stray!

The brothas under my window are blinded and lost, but Jesus made room for these men at the cross.

Maybe you have a window and a ear to hear the sound. Now open up your heart and watch God turn it all around.

So send I you to the boys around the way! Time to reach out lend a helping hand, Jesus will make a way.

Go ahead, they are waiting!

# Hugs Aren't Supposed to Hurt

Hugs aren't suppose to hurt, especially in the Body of Christ. Lord I don't understand why these hugs don't seem so very nice. Is it me am I just off, or are these hugs smothered in dirty cloths?

Father I just can't pretend that everything here is alright, something about that hug leaves me tossing and turning all times of night!

A camouflage to distort the truth, a blanket to cover my eyes. Is this hug just another way, from exposing just another lie? The truth of the matter is that you've taught me so much about your love. So I now recognize when the hug is sent from you Father from up above.

How can we say we love you, yet we're deceptive with a phony grin? Father I'm asking you to fix it! The cruelty and hatred must end! I'm asking you to open my heart and fix all that is wrong. Please help me to understand this hug that kept me up all night long!

Father you promised me sweet sleep, to stay up through the night is vain, but the tears refuse to stop raining and my heart can't shake this pain!

I'm casting my cares at your feet, help me to just leave them there. Because I'm safe in your arms, when I can't find comfort anywhere.

I love my brothers and sisters, mothers and fathers too, but hugs aren't suppose to hurt, so Lord what would you have me to do? Bless the ones that curse you? Obey those that have rule? Just because some are older, doesn't mean anyone's finished with school.

Endure hardness as a good soldier, wipe your eyes and you'll see, send up Judah and come closer. For I've given you the victory! There is no time to stay angry, wounded, or just in a cave. Time for you to start living new life, enjoying the promise I've made.

Remember I am your Father, I formed the eye and I see. Take up your cross daily. Continue to love and seek me. Your heart is very tender, I've placed my love in your touch. No hugs weren't made to hurt, but healing cost my Son Jesus so much!

Be wise as a serpent and guard your heart. Remember my love and never depart. Trust and believe I see all things. Continue to let my praises ring!

Nope, hugs aren't supposed to hurt!

Every time I try to understand exactly what's taken place.
The frustration and anger is just written all over my face.
It takes time to study and pray,
to realize the Lord doesn't do it our way.
A whole new language in a whole new world,
lots of life changing decisions and situations, but
the sweet Holy Spirit will give you mind blowing...

# REVELATIONS

You don't ask much for all you gave,
but for me to obey, trust and be saved.

Show up on time, read your word.
Stop all the worrying, look at the birds!
Forgive everyone, show up on time.
Repent, believe and drink this new wine!

Surrender, confess, yield and come close,
bow down and worship the Lord of host.
Read the Bible, study, rehearse.
Give thanks in everything, it could get worse!

Lift up Jesus, both day and night,
know that nothing shall separate me
from your love and light!

Give you the Glory and always pray.
Be sober and vigilant, humble myself and stay
closer and closer, nearer to the cross.
Where Jesus is Lord and no souls are lost!

Come out from amongst them,
seek your face, rejoice and press, keep the pace.

Surrender my will, practice, and be free,
know that all things are possible to him that believe.

Turn from the darkness, step into the light.
Practice and respond to your love and live right.

Father I do understand each one of these rules.
Yet I still get side tracked using your tools!

It takes so much focus, just to sit still.
Quiet myself and learn your will!

You truly are worthy, much more then a man.
I'm not giving up, each day I rely on your plans.
Jesus is Lord, I've just gotta win,
wash me in the blood again and again!

Feed me Father, til I want no more,
I'll touch no unclean thing, seal every door!
Continue to mend, my broken, shattered heart.
I declare and decree purity and a new start!
Father are you with me? With you I agree.

I'm calling out to you, because I've just gotta be free!

Once again I hear you,
you panic so much.
Trust and believe, I love you
and I'm hear to touch.

There is no more time to keep on going back,
you must be steadfast and stay on track!

Look at the lilies, now look at the birds.
My child write each and every vision,
you must do what you've heard!

You are in a new season and I want for you to relax.
All that has been taken, I'm here to give it back!

I'm giving you more joy, peace, and love,
I'm giving you increase, miracles from above.
Now don't you forget, cause it's gonna happen fast,
Jesus is Lord, only lifting Christ does last!

Give me the Glory for everything I do,
always obey and know that I am with you!

Relax!

King David and I had the honor to be a part of our brother and sister's wedding. We prepared for over a week, we were excited. Now these were not just our biological family.

This is our big brother and sister from the body of Christ. What do you know? Jesus did it again. Not only did He allow us to participate, but He gave us two friends.

Everyone who attended the wedding and the reception were very well fed.

As the groom and the bride became one, here's exactly what King David and I said at THE WEDDING/RECEPTION.

# THE WEDDING POEM

Let there be Jesus as our foundation, as we lift Him each day.
Let there be love and commitment that would cause us not to
stray.

Let there be joy and peace as we both strive to do our parts.
Let there be trust one for another as we choose never to
depart.

Let there be unity and communication as the days tend
to grow long. Let there be truth and understanding when
everything seems to go wrong.

Let there be confidence, you above all others I have preferred.
Let there be resilience to resolve matters of great gravity, or
most absurd.

Let there be laughter and forgiveness as we walk as one in
this new day. Let there be listening and long suffering as we
endure and we pray.

Let there be transparency from one another, we do not have
to hide. Let there be compassion when in one another we
confide.

Let there be friendship and a connection, intimacy enough. Let there be wisdom and respect as the road ahead can sometimes get rough.

Let there be patience with one another enduring each and every test. Let there be gentleness in our words, seasoned with salt is best.

Let us remember this decision and these vows with no compromise. Let us give God all the glory as we join not to divide.

Let us hold fast to all of God's promises , to produce not to decay. Let us take heed to every word God says, to perform it without delay.

Let there be joy on our journey,let us stand on God's word. Let there be power and provision, let us do what we've heard.

Let there be healing and wholeness with grateful hearts. What God has joined together, let no man tear apart.

# THE RECEPTION

We outta here at least by nine,
not watching ya car
cause Sharon looking fine!
Kids at home chillin
and that's alright with me.
My Lord, and my wife will agree.

Thanks for coming out
to celebrate this day,
but it's time for the honeymoon
so get outta my way.

We have crossed over
to the other side.
Thank you Jesus for how you've
kept our dream alive.

We had to fast, focus,
you know we had to pray,
for every step that led us here today.

We thank you for the love
gathered in this room.
Gimme a kiss honey
cuz we already jumped the broom!
I'm with you honey,

let's not be late.
I put a little celery
on your plate.

I'm your sugar and so
you won't miss out.
We can rest for a season.
Jesus moved the stress and doubt.

It's time for us to dance,
let me see that smile.
This moment we've been
waiting for took a little while.

Our family and friends
we do appreciate,
but you must go home
cuz it's a half past eight.

I get a little serious
when it comes to my man.
Jesus has blessed us.
Hope you all understand.

We really love you all so much,
no time for gloom and doom.
Ya heard what my husband said,
"We just jumped the broom!"

We love you Brother Karl, and Sister Sharon.

It feels so great this new life I now live. God is just so amazing, look at what He's chosen to give.

The love of Jesus... He's taught me so much over many years, but when you've been traumatized so much just disappears.

God gave me so much mercy paired with heapings of grace. Dispatched His representatives to help me run this race.

I'm celebrating each lesson and all the training you still choose to give, and I give you all the glory because...

# I'm Learning to Live

This is something that I've never even tried. Since the age of eight I just wanted to die! Couldn't find a reason to stick around. Every human in my life just tried to beat me down.

Bit by a dog at the age of three. From four to five in surgery. In a hit and run I crossed at the light!

I was ten years old out in the cold. I loved everybody, but they just hated me! Didn't know I had a Savior that died for me.

They beat me in school, beat me at home. Didn't take much to see I was on my own! So in the streets I wandered and roamed.

They cut off my hair, force fed me too, jammed glass in my elbow, beat me black and blue. They beat me all day and half through the night. Cut open my thumb with an electric carving knife.

Out in the snow with no shoes or a coat, the neighbors all laughed. I had no place to go! They took me to church and beat me there too, they said I was bad, but exactly what did I do?

At nine years old they beat me some more, called me a liar, a tramp and a whore. I ran to the church again and again, but they just prayed and sent me right back in!

I called out to God, but He wasn't there, I hated Him, too. He didn't even care. He watched them folks all have a turn. It's when I got to Bethel I started to learn. Now this process has taken many years, I'm not finish yet, but over these years...

I've learned to wash up and make a bed, Jesus has taught me to lift up my head. I wash my clothes and I've stopped lying, too. There's just no limit to what Jesus can do! I'm learning to think, I can even sit still, no doctors, drugs, and never any pills!

Jesus made a way outta no way and so I've been sent and I'm compelled to say please don't give up. Throw hatred away.

Keep coming back. Sit under God's word. How can you learn if you haven't even heard? Yes, you've heard a lot, but I'm talking about the Truth. Jesus kept me, so here is your proof!

God is love. We have no excuse to continue in a life with a dead end. Come to Jesus and start over again!

It's not too late and it's not to hard, Jesus completed the race. He ran the last yard! "Just show up," like Pastor Lambert said. God will do the rest, Jesus can raise the dead!

I'm learning to live.

So many testimonies, so many stories, so many times.

God must get the Glory, be it morning, noon, or night
but He's given me the...

# BRAGGIN RIGHTS

My life is not the same.
My mind is being changed.
Not looking back no more.
I'm confident and sure!
Eating manna everyday
Still learning what to say.

Jesus filled my cup,
and has taught me to look up!
Even in this pain
with no one to explain.

He cleansed me from those stains.
Removed defeat and shame,
without that worldly gain.
But I'm richer than ever before,
not sleeping on the floor no more,
and even if I did,
my life has now been hid!

A blood bath everyday.
Instead of fighting with my hands,
now I'm learning how to pray!
Standing on God's word,
I'm now doing what I heard.
Starting school again,
cause Jesus is my friend
Who sticks much closer than a brother
He stayed when I had no mother,
and my father left me too?

So Lord this shoutout's just for you!

My King of kings, and my Lord of lords,
my shelter and my sounding board!
My source, my help, and all my strength,
my Holy redeemer and my night watchman.
My shield, my guide, my buckler,
my teacher and my councilor,
I'm thinking now, mind regulator!

Alpha, and Omega, so thankful for what you gave!
Another chance for me,
with you Holy Spirit I bow, and agree!
No more looking down, nor shouting out the blues.
Instead I'm spreading God's great news!
That Jesus died and rose again,
saved me from, death and sin.

He snatched those keys,
He robbed deaths grave!
So get on up and lets try again,
Jesus blotted out that sin!
No more condemnation,
you're a chosen generation.
So show your appreciation.
No, not to me! Christ made us free!
No more backing up,
let Jesus fill your cup!
Over, and over, again and again,
He's my living water there is no end!

To what my Savior can do,
He's no respecter of persons.

He'll save and keep you too!
Just call upon His name and
in your heart believe,
be honest and tell the truth,
and you too shall receive!

He is my rereward,
so now I'm marching towards
my final destination.
There is no limitation
to what my Lord can do.

So yield and watch Jesus
see you through.
Now is not the time
for us to turn away,
for we are not our own,
a sacrifice was made!

Way back on Calvary Jesus paid it all,
for when you're down and dirty
or standing proud and tall!
So bless His Holy name,
He's worthy to be praised.
Jesus requires a life change,
not a twenty four hour phase!

So help me lift Jesus higher,
He is the soon coming Messiah!
Praise is free, you don't have
to buy a tape, CD, or song,
you can praise His name
when you're weak or strong!
Jesus made it all alright and
left me with these braggin rights!

Do you realize that no matter what's going down that JESUS died and rose again for us to have a mind that's strong and sound?

Jesus bled and died, endured it all way back on Calvary. No matter who rejects the Gospel, I know He did it...

When I write Lord is it you, or just some phase I must go through? What about the hearers, or the vocabulary I choose?

When they think I'm being smart, or have a bad attitude. How will I explain the things that I must say and what about the people who turn and walk away?

Lord I really need you as I learn to use this gift, please Lord help me to interpret, through all my words please sift? Forgive me for being lazy and not giving my all to you. Here I am my Father ready to hear your point of view.

I need you every second, my life is in your hands. With your love, power, and soundness of mind I'm ready to hear your plans. I need to hear your heart Lord, please speak and help me to obey, I really need a lot of help each and everyday!

So I bow down my ear Lord sitting at your feet. Realizing I just can't write, I must wait to hear you speak. My daughter hear I am, you are not alone, I sit high, I'm holding your hand as I sit upon my throne.

You have been given this talent, now you must be secure. I've wrapped your heart with so much love, it's nothing like you've had before.
My people they will hear you, my sheep they do hear my voice. Set your face like flint, be still and just rejoice!

Many of my children are waiting, you must trust and believe, that your loving father is with you and has given you the victory! You'll never please all the people and this is not your task, I will strengthen your tender heart every time you ask.

You must quiet down now, take some time and rest. Make sure that you read my word and you will always be blessed.

Now you have your answer, this ones just for you. Pull it out this poem that is whenever you feel afraid.

Just keep on writing my heart and remember the promise I've made. So now you know I'm with you. Stop running and turning away.

Hold my hand tight, lift up your voice even when you feel slayed! See I know many have hurt you and made you feel ashamed, put a blanket on all of their wrong, so you'd take on all the blame.

I will help you forgive, surrender each one from your heart, I watched them tare you again and again each time I gave you a new start.

Today is your new beginning I've come to take all the pain weariness in well doing, keep your mind from going insane.

I'm here to vindicate you, I'm restoring you in this day. Remember to continue reading your word and always stop to pray. Lean not to your own understanding, many times you have been wrong. Be slow to speak I'll protect you, keep singing your new songs.

My daughter I adore you, great is my mercy in your life, I want you to practice and be prepared free from worry and strife.

Consecrate yourself, sanctified I'm here for you. Love has been your just reward I've given my all to you.

Stop beating up on yourself, just because you make mistakes. Haven't you notice how you repent and you're not fake?

Okay I've lifted your spirit, the world is in my hands. With you my darling daughter I've shared so many of my plans.

Remember to forgive your family, each and everyone. Remember how I have forgiven you.

Remember Jesus my Son!

I had to take some time out.

You know, to take a good look at me. Not in the mirror, but deep down within. Had to cry out to Jesus.

He gave good direction. He shined His light in my soul, as I did an...

# INTROSPECTION

Am I sewing discord, jealous and just mad? Envious and in a rage cause of what others seem to have?

When I look back over my life, do I like the view, or am I stuck on rewind , just checking out who is who?

Am I hypocritical, and always holding a grudge, acting like I'm on TV, like I'm some famous judge?

Am I just so bitter, that Mara has become my name, and instead of seeking Jesus, I've been seeking riches and fame?

Is my heart still broken, and unable to be fixed? Because instead of laying down prostrate, I'm throwing stones and sticks?

Jesus I'm so tired of staying up half the night, angry, cussing and crying, so mad I'm just ready to fight!

I heard that you would heal me, if I would let go and repent. Spend some time in your presence, just start all over again!

Your mercy endures forever, you'll bare my burdens please, fill me with the Holy Ghost and safely lead me out!

You are my deliverer, the lover of my soul. Jesus here I am knocking, please come and make me whole!

Give it to me, I'll bare it, lean on me cause I'm your rock. I'll even mend all that's broken, I'm your great physician, you can call me Doc!

This road hasn't been easy, my child you must forgive.
Stay a while in my presence, I will teach you how to live.
Your life is far from over.

Just cast your cares on me. Remember that I am your
watchmen, and I've given you the victory!

Thank you Jesus!

It just takes too much time and energy dwelling on yesterday. Most of the trouble I've had in my life never even happened! Yes, bad things occurred all the time, but at times I anticipated the worst and by the time I had the courage to confront the situation at hand, it was already worked out.

My life and circumstances never surprised God! Nothing that has taken place, nor any upcoming events will ever separate any of us from the love of my Lord and Savior JESUS CHRIST.

My life is in His hands. Well life...

# It Went The Way It Was Supposed To Go

I could'a did this and I should'a did that, that's all I keep hearing when I focused on looking back. If I would'a tried, it might have all worked out, but whatever happened to believing God and casting down all doubt.

God made away, out of no way . So when I look back over my life, how can I sit and say?

My life is a mistake and something happened well that was fake. This talk calls God a liar, and it's his heart we break.

He really is the potter and we truly are His clay. God molded us and shaped us and He's still at work this day!

I thought to write this poem to let my brothers and sisters know, stop crying and feeling guilty cause it went the way it was suppose to go!

Every footstep you made is ordered God has written out your path. Unbelief calls him a liar and you'll be subjected to his wrath.

If you don't believe me just read it for yourself, but we suffer from a lack of knowledge, but Jesus He is our help. All things are working together and it's working for your good. Even when you've been rejected and always misunderstood.

I've never met my family and I had no history. Couldn't even trace my blood line, nor draw my family tree!

Ate scraps out the trash. Was never first but last. Slept on sidewalks, hid in a bush. Most of my life just over looked! See I went to work at the age of ten, tears day and night.

I really had no friends and the neighbors they just laughed like this was some kinda show, but I'm now walking in God's forgiveness, cause it went the way it was supposed to go!

I was very, very angry, cause they even changed my name. From Kiami Carter to Crystal Kirk, but who was there to blame?

I'm now thankful for this story and even all life's pain, cause if I didn't suffer I could never reign!

Suffering oh yes! It truly is a must. So go ahead and take life's lumps and remember in God we trust.

They stamped that on our money, but it's truly what God has said, remember He gave His only Son. Jesus His only Begotten Son. Who suffered, died, and bled!

Now this is not the end, cause Jesus rose again. So go on through, but come on out, only believe Jesus worked it out!

Don't get sad, stop feeling all bad, when you stop to reflect don'tcha even get mad!

Just remember Jesus is running this show, and your life, well it went the way it's supposed to go!

Walking in a wilderness day after day. Back and forth in my mind, keep jumping off track. Not a substance or a vice could ever bring me back.

All of this depression worries me. I'm making a new choice time to let you know...

# MY MIND IS MADE UP

I've made up my mind
to put hatred down.
You gave me a new life and
I'm not backing down.
You gave clear instructions
right here in your word,
so I choose to obey
and apply all I've heard.

You are my Father
and you gave me your all,
when you gave your Son Jesus
so I can stand tall!

It wasn't in vain,
all that you've done.
The battle has been fought,
the victory is won.
So I've made up my mind
to see through your eyes,
to take up my cross
even when I'm despised!

I refuse to turn away
when the road gets rough,
or when I'm all messed up
and situations get tough!

I've made up my mind
to believe you anyway,

to listen and be quiet,
when I have more to say.

Even when I'm right
in my own heart,
I'm laying it down
from your love I won't depart!

Jesus you are Lord,
our soon coming King,
so instead of complaining,
your praises I'll sing!

Lord you suffered long,
and you did nothing wrong,
so I've made up my mind
to keep singing this love song!

I'm asking for your help,
I welcome you in,
I thank you for your blood
to cleanse me from all sin.

I don't want to betray you,
nor walk in my own way.
Holy Spirit you are welcome,
come teach me how to pray.

I've made up my mind
to lift your precious name,

this is a declaration.
I will not be ashamed.

My brothers and sisters,
you can join me too.
Just make up your mind.
Jesus cares for you!

You don't have to be perfect
to make a new choice.
Pick up God's word,
and learn to hear His voice.

Make up your mind
to call upon His name.
Jesus is a present help
in this world of pain!

So come out from among them,
separate yourself.
God will bring you out
into a place of wealth.


A wealthy place
when you make up your mind.
Answer when God calls.
We're running out of time!

The day you hear my voice, harden not your heart.

You know what the Lord has been faithful to all humanity.
Gave His only Son that we could have life more abundantly.
No more time to sit on the sideline day after day,
WHEN THE LORD Jesus Christ is well on the way.
Stand up, repent, walk in His power.
The Lord has issued a warning...


THE HOUR IS COMING that no man can work!

# The Hour is Coming

Mice climb in my bed,
roaches crawling over my head,
babies stomping on the ceiling
loud enough to wake the dead!
Pain running up my back,
gotta glue back in this track,
junkies and dealers in the neighborhood
selling and cooking crack!

Buy cheese from the papis
that don't melt, baby daddy
ain't strong enough to help,
insensitive people with lots of opinions
don't even know how it felt.
Momma put me out
at the tender age of ten.
Senior citizens shaking their heads
because they don't know where I been.

Phone bill due today,
electric bill on the way,
winter's coming,
fridge on the blitz
and the church on the corner
said they'll pray!
Well I read that Bible too.
You supposed to show love and do.
Stop asking a million questions
tryna hear about what I've been through!

Turn that music down,
open up your ears!
You're blind from all that
religious stuff you been practicing
all of these years.
Jesus died for me, even if you disagree,
cause you been saved for
over twenty years still
acting like a pharisee!

Lying won't get you in,
smiling ova ya sin,
back biting and gossiping
cause you think you're making it in!
Jesus came for the lost
to set the captives free.
The ones who have been broken
and bruised,
He's given us the victory!

That man laying on that vent
was truly heaven sent
but you walked by and shook your head
cause you had to get to some event!
That family that needed some food,
but you're not in the mood
and since it's not Sunday morning,
you give out your attitude!

Today is a new day,
another chance for you to stop
wearing those shirts and those hats
asking what would Jesus do!
Give out some of those clothes,
pocket books, and those shoes.
Stop complaining about your life
and go spread God's great news!

Time is no one's friend,
be careful how you spend.
Life is but a vapor and
it could bring you a tragic end!
Hey, you up on the front row!
I just thought you should know
exactly what the Lord meant when
He said, "get up and go."

You act like you can't hear,
with your fancy clothes and those hats.
Pride comes before a fall.
You better watch where you've been sat!
We've all been sent with a purpose,
we all have something to do.
So I'mma get focused and busy.
I suggest you do the same thing too!

The hour is coming when no man can work!

I'm determined now more than ever. I continue to focus on the trials test and tribulations, the pain, heart aches, the grief and the world putting on a great show.

I've made up my mind...

# I'm Not Letting Go

The oil on my hands called abuse. The bitterness in my heart to form an excuse.

The terror in my eye from all that I've seen. The murder on display to crush my childhood dreams.

The people in high places putting on a great show, I've gotta news flash I'm not letting go!

My heart has been busted even at my own hand, my knees have given way making it difficult to stand.

My heart is beating fast, my pulse is faint and slow, no matter the report still I'm not letting go!

Arteries clogged from years of pain, legs feel like jello, trouble on my brain!

Look outta the window what is it that I see, twenty different cults try'na grab a hold of me!

A Muslim right here, Catholics on the end, Watchtowers on my steps, headlines read, "we'll help you make it in!"


Baptist on the news, here comes the Church of God and Christ, Latter day Saints with their bowties tied just right!

Buddha on the floor, I just want you all to know, no matter what the religious trips I'm still not letting go!

Now let's wrap it all up with your local assembly, hollering and screaming how Jesus came to set us all free, then why you still wearing a mask pointing ya fingers at me?

You said that I could make it, that Jesus paid it all, but when people come in and don't do it your way, you can't wait to see us fall!

If I sound a little angry, I'm tired of all I see. We put a title on rotten fruit, smile, and just agree!

I've been under great attacks, circumstance has slowed my flow. My Lord and Savior held me tight, so I'm not letting go!

Now I'm a little older, I know that Jesus has a plan. Keep your eyes on Jesus, the rock of all ages. He'll help you to stand!

Trials, persecution, and suffering all helps you to grow. No matter what may come my way, still I'm not letting go!

I'm so glad God has taken these blinders off of my mind! He has placed a level of appreciation in me.

So when I get a glimpse of God's power in the earth, it causes me to exhale, to even breathe again!

Open my eyes, oh Lord, that I may behold wondrous things out of thy law.

Thank you Lord for dwelling amongst us and allowing us to see your power and glory manifested in the earth.

JESUS IS ALIVE!!!

I SEE YOU!

# HE'S ALIVE

I'm still alive, thought I'd be dead after all the millions of times I've been bust in the head!

I'm still alive, but I've waited to die. Dehydrated and famished living in the lies.

First and second degree burns eating at my flesh. Mental torment to finish off the rest.

That tuna can that cut deep into my face. The glass jammed in my elbow as I bled all over the place.

I'm still alive after eating scraps outta the trash and the millions of times I broke out from colds and rash. Those little white worms nearly ate me alive, I never got treated at twelve I still just waited to die!

Those headaches that hurt for over three to four days, the people that said I suffered because of my own ways.

The surgeries that hurt and caused me to pee, I never wet the bed until those doctors discharged me.

The men that raped me when I was underage, at twelve or thirteen, I was filled with so much rage!

That marble ashtray they used to crack my head, those that gossiped and laughed and left me for dead, but I'm still alive and yes I'm still surprised because diseases ran through my body and truly I never tried.

How could this be? What answer could I give?
I must truly tell you I made no effort to live.

One day someone told me that for God so loved the world,
that He gave His only Begotten Son to save a sin sick world!
That if I would confess and welcome Jesus in my heart, He
would give me life and I would be a part.

So I opened up my mouth and I truly believed. He washed me
in the precious blood and set my soul free!

So here I am today, Jesus paid it all. God had a purpose and a
plan. He gave me life ya'll!

So this life I now live doesn't belong to me, I now live for my
Lord and Savior who sets the captive free!

# Baby You Better Think About It

Baby you better think about it,
because sin is knocking at your door.
Satan is searching to and fro,
playtime is over. This is war!

He's looking for young brothers
and he wants our sisters too.
He's watching and he's waiting
until this class is through.

Did you do your homework?
Have you studied for the test?
Or did you blow it off
just like all of the rest?

I know you've had to notice
the sex and profanity,
not just in the schools,
but it's all over the TV.

Earrings in their mouths,
thongs way up your back, and you're
representatives of Jesus Christ.
What kind of rep is that?

Some are getting high and
dropping out of school.
Rebellion is on the rampage and
they're breaking all of the rules.

Sex is on the menu
in this world, it's just a mess.
Children giving up their bodies
cause they feel they're second best!

It's a lie when Satan tells you,
"You must try it just one time."
At first he'll take your body, and then
he comes to snatch your mind.

Diseases in your body
and a baby on the way,
because instead of praying about it,
you thought it was okay.

You came out to this class and
I hope that you have learned
why it's better to marry.
See hell is hot and you will burn!

Jesus is your help,
He'll show up right on time.
Your body belongs to Jesus.
He's paid the price for you and I.

The precious Blood of Jesus
has given us the victory!

Listen to your parents,
even when they work your nerves.
Surrender your life to Jesus.
You can take Him at His word.

Life won't always be easy,
but you know we need you.
So before you make decisions,
baby you better think it through!

God will send you someone
who will listen and hold your hand.
Happiness is not from a girlfriend
or from a one night stand.

God has given you life and
He made you for Himself,
not for fleshy idols, sex, and drugs,
riches, or for wealth.

Yes, there's lots of pressure,
trouble comes to make you strong,
and God has given His word
so we do know right from wrong.

Before you take that chance and
you feel like you just can't stand,
call a brother or a sister
who will lend a helping hand!

As I stand here before you
I'm so proud of what I see,
you finished out this program
a part of God's strategy.

Don't allow this to be the end,
please make up your mind.
When the devil comes to try you
You better think about it this time!

Nothing's gonna stop all that I see, before I was born it was given to me. I think about it, and I've always written it down. If you don't write the vision your dreams will just drown.

I've had to pray often and I've had to do much work. With God, and Jesus no matter how circumstances seem I just didn't let go of the vision and THE DREAM.

# THE DREAM

I've had the same dream since the age of eight.
Since I'm still alive it's not to late.

The earth will hear me as I turn each page,
I'm refusing to stay stuck , loud and in a rage.

Handmaid and Company, each of my books,
every song with it's delivering hook.

The classes I'll teach to lift up hung down heads.
As I spread the gospel of how Jesus hung, died, and bled!

I'll preach Christ crucified at every show.
I'm on my way to Carnegie Hall to let the others know.

I'm gonna paint God's love on the hearts of man.
With this new life I'm moving just as fast as I can.

The foods, the paints, the jewelry too.
Each poem written and a new way to choose.

Jesus is alive and so is my dream.
My husband and I aren't finished with our dreams.


A wellness center for children to grow,
I must give back, you see, it's time for me to sow.

All of the seeds God put in my hand,
my dreams and my destiny are all a part of God's plan.

My products will sell all over this world,
brightening the hearts of men, women, and many boys and girls.

I'm leaving a legacy. My life hasn't been in vain.
Jesus is Lord and your Kingdom doth rule and reign!

So many of God's leaders paved the way.
They were whipped and beaten and suffered many decades.
They marched, picked cotton, still letting God's praises ring...

that's why I HAVE A DREAM, just like Martin Luther King.

# I HAVE A DREAM

I have a dream, and so did Martin Luther King.
Martin believed God, and started doing his thing.

The Alabama March, the speech on the hill,
Martin laid down his life and started doing God's will.

He left his family at home.
He endured as the crowd through those rocks.
He lifted up Jesus daily and protested on many blocks.

Birmingham was dangerous, yet Martin never fought.
He picked up his cross daily,
knowing the battle was won and fought.

Martin showed up at the meetings,
never missing without a trace.
He said why sit here til I die and
let my dream just be erased?

They through him in prison, Martin had to bleed,
but like Paul and Silas, he praised God and agreed.

Jail couldn't hold him, because Jesus already told them that
many would go free, and that He was there to uphold him.

Truth had to be told. Martin had to be bold.
He didn't look at the task and say Lord , I'm just too old.

Martin had to look to Jesus, and so do you and I.
Stop all this giving up wondering who and why.

Grab hold of your vision, surrender your will to Christ.
Jesus is soon to return in a twinkling of an eye.

Grab hold of your vision, destiny dipped in dare.
Shake off all that self pity, God will lead you there.

God's word is a lamp, a light unto your feet.
He promised to be with you, he'll give you what to speak.

The love of Jesus will lift you, religion will let you down.
Surrender it all like Martin Luther King
and watch God turn it all around.

Religion equals division, Jesus equals love.
That's why Jesus was sent to restore us to our Father up above.

Before I end this poem, I'm compelled to let you know.
Only what we do for Christ will last.
Destiny starts when we let go.


In Christ do we live and move, and have our being.

# God's Favor

All along this winding road Lord you assisted me with each heavy load. Each time you hid me out, when I had no place to stay. All the many jail trips that were due to come my way.

That time on Fortieth and Market when I should've lost my mind, or how about that pimp that purchased all those clothes, yet I escaped just in the knick of time!

Those worms that invaded my body and I could've just fallen dead. Or how about all those folks that beat me upside my head! Those spelling bees I won at an early age. How about how you delivered me from sickness, hatred, and rage.

The jobs I've had with no diplomas or degrees, or the adults and many people who laughed when I was bound and lived in misery. How about how you have lifted my head and gave me so many gifts. Just so I could give you the Glory as you prepared me for this amazing shift!

I'm a cook, but I had no kitchen, a teacher without a degree, sheltered without a home, Lord you've been so good to me. I've shopped with next to no money, ran down three flights of stairs on next to no breath?

All the while I've learned it was your grace and mercy, you said, "Hold on for this is just your process!"

The trips and places to live, I've had more lives than Felix the cat. This favor you've placed on my life, Thank you Lord Jesus nothing could ever be greater than that!

I'm highly favored, there's just no doubt from then until now you've Blessed my soul, Lord Jesus, you've worked each chapter out. I'm grateful and blessed, never ashamed to say, Thank you Lord and Savior. Truly I can say unmerited favor you've placed it on my life.

Jesus is Lord and has turned the darkness to light.

God you're faithful!

So many of us trained in this class. We studied and practiced, this was just no easy task. Stand up straight, learn how to speak, show up on time week after week. Use all of your manners, and if you trip or fall get up because you're on your way to the princess ball...

# I'm A Princess

I didn't know this before,
I was defeated, hopeless and poor,
but nonetheless without a dress.
I'm a princess.

Ate right out of your plate,
my lifestyle was second rate.
Hatred and pain burden and drained,
but I'm a princess!

Wet the bed, hung down head.
When you saw me you were sure to dread,
living like the walking dead,
but I'm a princess.

No shoes, no coat,
no place to go.
Light the weed, pass the flow,
but I'm a princess!

My mentor told me years ago
before that day
I just didn't know
that I'm a princess.

She opened her door, gave me a bed,
held my hand and gently said,
"No matter what you've been through,
Jesus died to see you through."

This is not your destination,
just a challenging situation.

Jesus died and rose again,
so let's start over it's not the end.
We've got lots of work to do,
but first we must start with you.

I fought. I cried and wondered why.
Was lazy and doubted and always lied,
I turned away a many of day,
yet I could always hear my mentor say
that I'm still a princess.

Shaking and shouting,
always pouting,
still, I'm a princess!

I fought every step of the way.
This process was painful,
but I'm here today.
Many years later,
I'm not done at all,
but I'm on my way
to the princess ball.

I was never God's second best
with or without a frilly dress.
God sent me there so I could tell you
how much Jesus cares and loves you too!

You have to get up,
no sleeping around!
Button your blouse,
stop looking down!

Comb your hair,
wash your face.
Be patient,
Jesus won this race!

Eat the right foods,
brush your teeth too.
It's a lot, but you can do
all that God said.
You must read your Word,
no more self pity,
do all that you've heard!

You'll fall and cry
and scrape your knees
but get back up.
You've got the victory!

Ms. B is helping with
the transformation.
Just a shout out
of appreciation.

When she's sick and feeling down,
Ms. B. always sticks around.

You've loved us all and we love you.
We all thank God for sending you.

Don't give up.
Don't look down.
Satan's a liar.
Drown out that sound.

It's a lot, but God
will give you rest.
So remember life is
a series of tests.

Pass or fail,
nonetheless,
you are God's princess!

# About the Author
# End Time Poet

End Time Poet is my name.
I was born to lift up Jesus' name.
The road I've traveled was hard and rough,
I had to surrender because enough was enough!
My head was hung low, my mind was a mess,
I really hated God and this whole process.

I'm a witness of God's power and love.
He transformed my life, lifted my head
When circumstance and humanity left me for dead.
I've made bad choices, I was just to loud.
Instead of loving Jesus, I followed the crowd.
This is my story and I'm not turning back.
It was the love of Jesus who brought me back.

Some of you met me
and saw me at my worst,
but I've got the victory!
GOD put it in reverse!

I love the Lord, He heard my cry!
I've found my seat at Jesus' feet.

Amen

# About the Publisher Sovereign Noir

Sovereign Noir Publications believes that every Black woman has a story to tell and that it should be done as professionally, intentionally, and unapologetically as possible.

Sovereign Noir has published dozens of books for Black women writers across the United States in addition to launching the Sovereign Noir Publications Annual Black Women Writers Virtual Summit and partnering with Friendship Charter Schools to provide the Sovereign Noir and Yolonda D. Coleman Writing Awards.

Sovereign Noir Publications is a company that brings boldness and authority to Black women writers by providing a high-quality book publishing experience. Connect with us at www.sovereignnoir.com, or on Instagram and Facebook @sovereign.noir.